STATIONS

—

G000277564

JOHN HENRY NEWMAN

FAMILY PUBLICATIONS

OXFORD

ISBN 978-1-871217-89-6

Art credits

Cover: © Bibliothèques d'Amiens Métropole,
Ms 154 C, fol 139v, Cliché IRHT-CNRS
Page 1: © Ville du Mans. Médiathèque Louis-Aragon, Ms 223, fol 135v
Page 3: © Bibliothèque Municipale Classée d'Autun, S 99 A, fol 140, Cliché IRHT-CNRS
Station I: © Bibliothèque municipale Georges-Pompidou de Châlons-en-Champagne,
Ms 336, fol 45, Cliché IRHT-CNRS
Station II: © Ville du Mans. Médiathèque Louis-Aragon, Ms 688, fol 41
Station III: © BMVR Marseille : Ms 89 Speculum humanae salvationis, fol 22v :
Montée au calvaire, Cliché IRHT-CNRS
Station IV: © Bibliothèque municipale de Tours, Ms 218, fol 62v, Cliché IRHT-CNRS
Station V: Toulouse, © Bibliothèque municipale, Ms 135, fol 68, Ph. G. Boussières
Station VI: © Bibliothèque municipale de Chaumont, Ms 34, fol 31v, Cliché IRHT-CNRS
Station VII: © Bibliothèque de Riom communauté, Ms 76, fol 53, Cliché IRHT–CNRS
Station VIII: © Bibliothèque municipale Livrée Ceccano, Avignon, Ms 136, fol 310v,
Cliché IRHT-CNRS
Station IX: © Bibliothèque Sainte-Geneviève, Paris, Ms 106, fol 90, Cliché IRHT-CNRS
Station X: © Bibliothèque municipale d'Abbeville, Ms 16, fol 28, Cliché IRHT-CNRS
Station XI: © Bibliothèque municipale de Dijon, Ms 2245, fol 59, Ph. E. Juvin
Station XII: © Bibliothèque municipale de Dijon, Ms 2244, fol 24, Ph. E. Juvin
Station XIII: © Bibliothèque municipale Livrée Ceccano, Avignon, Ms 121, fol 55v,
Cliché IRHT-CNRS
Station XIV: © Bibliothèque municipale de Chaumont, Ms 34, fol 41v, Cliché IRHT-CNRS
Page 32: Folio 259v, Trône de grâce, Manuscrit 21, Guillaud Durand, Rational des Divins
Offices, 15ème siècle © Bibliothèque Gaspard Monge, Ville de Beaune

Original text used with permission of the Fathers of the Birmingham Oratory

published by
Family Publications
Denis Riches House, 66 Sandford Lane
Kennington, Oxford, OX1 5RP
www.familypublications.co.uk

printed in Malta by Melita Press
through s|s|media ltd

✠

The Stations of the Cross begin with an Act of Contrition:

O my God, because thou art so good, I am very sorry that I have sinned against thee and with the help of thy grace I will not sin again.

Amen.

☙

At the beginning of each station:

℣. *We adore thee O Christ and we bless thee.*
℞. *Because by thy Holy Cross thou hast redeemed the world.*

☙

At the conclusion of each station:

Our Father, Hail Mary, Glory be

℣. *Have mercy on us O Lord.*
℞. *Have mercy on us.*

May the souls of the faithful departed through the mercy of God rest in peace.

☙

Between stations, a verse of the Stabat Mater, printed underneath the illustration for each station, may be said or sung.

At the Cross her station keeping,
Stood the mournful Mother weeping
Close to Jesus to the last.

Jesus is condemned to Death

℣. *We adore thee O Christ and we bless thee.*

℟. *Because by thy Holy Cross thou hast redeemed the world.*

The Holy, Just, and True was judged by sinners, and put to death. Yet, while they judged, they were compelled to acquit Him. Judas, who betrayed Him, said, "I have sinned in that I have betrayed the innocent blood." Pilate, who sentenced Him, said, "I am innocent of the blood of this just person," and threw the guilt upon the Jews. The Centurion who saw Him crucified said, "Indeed this *was* a just man." Thus ever, O Lord, Thou art justified in Thy words, and dost overcome when Thou art judged. And so, much more, at the last day "They shall *look* on Him whom they pierced" ; and He who was condemned in weakness shall judge the world in power, and even those who are condemned will confess their judgment is just.

Our Father, Hail Mary, Glory be ...

℣. *Have mercy on us O Lord...*

Through her heart His sorrow sharing
All His bitter anguish bearing,
Now at length the sword had passed.

Second station

Jesus receives His Cross

℣. *We adore thee O Christ and we bless thee.*

℟. *Because by thy Holy Cross thou hast redeemed the world.*

Jesus supports the whole world by His divine power, for He is God; but the weight was less heavy than was the Cross which our sins hewed out for Him. Our sins cost Him this humiliation. He had to take on Him our nature, and to appear among us as a man, and to offer up for us a great sacrifice. He had to pass a life in penance, and to endure His passion and death at the end of it. O Lord God Almighty, who dost bear the weight of the whole world without weariness, who bore the weight of all our sins, though they wearied Thee, as Thou art the Preserver of our bodies by Thy Providence, so be Thou the Saviour of our souls by Thy precious blood.

Our Father, Hail Mary, Glory be ...

℣. *Have mercy on us O Lord...*

O how sad and sore distressed
Was that Mother highly blessed,
Of the sole begotten One!

THIRD STATION

JESUS FALLS UNDER THE WEIGHT OF THE CROSS THE FIRST TIME

℣. *We adore thee O Christ and we bless thee.*

℟. *Because by thy Holy Cross thou hast redeemed the world.*

SATAN fell from heaven in the beginning; by the just sentence of his Creator he fell, against whom he had rebelled. And when he had succeeded in gaining man to join him in his rebellion, and his Maker came to save him, then his brief hour of triumph came, and he made the most of it. When the Holiest had taken flesh, and was in his power, then in his revenge and malice he determined, as he himself had been struck down by the Almighty arm, to strike in turn a heavy blow at Him who struck him. Therefore it was that Jesus fell down so suddenly. O dear Lord, by this Thy first fall raise us all out of sin, who have so miserably fallen under its power.

Our Father, Hail Mary, Glory be ...

℣. *Have mercy on us O Lord...*

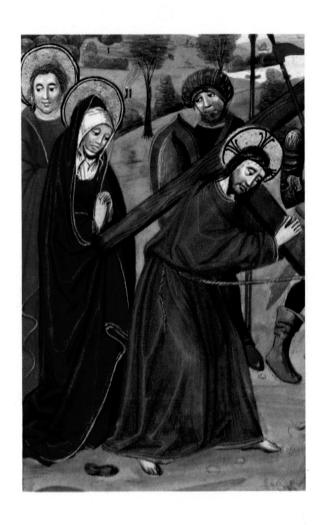

Christ above in torment hangs,
She beneath beholds the pangs
Of her dying glorious Son.

JESUS MEETS HIS MOTHER

℣. *We adore thee O Christ and we bless thee.*

℟. *Because by thy Holy Cross thou hast redeemed the world.*

THERE is no part of the history of Jesus but Mary has her part in it. There are those who profess to be His servants, who think that her work was ended when she bore Him, and after that she had nothing to do but disappear and be forgotten. But we, O Lord, Thy children of the Catholic Church, do not so think of Thy Mother. She brought the tender Infant into the Temple, she lifted Him up in her arms when the wise men came to adore Him. She fled with Him to Egypt, she took Him up to Jerusalem when He was twelve years old. He lived with her at Nazareth for thirty years. She was with Him at the marriage-feast. Even when He had left her to preach, she hovered about Him. And now she shows herself as He toils along the Sacred Way with His cross on His shoulders. Sweet Mother, let us ever think of thee when we think of Jesus, and when we pray to Him, ever aid us by thy powerful intercession.

Our Father, Hail Mary, Glory be ...

℣. *Have mercy on us O Lord...*

Is there one who would not weep,
Whelmed in miseries so deep
Christ's dear Mother to behold?

SIMON OF CYRENE HELPS JESUS TO CARRY THE CROSS

℣. *We adore thee O Christ and we bless thee.*

℟. *Because by thy Holy Cross thou hast redeemed the world.*

JESUS could bear His Cross alone, did He so will; but He permits Simon to help Him, in order to remind us that we must take part in His sufferings, and have a fellowship in His work. His merit is infinite, yet He condescends to let His people add their merit to it. The sanctity of the Blessed Virgin, the blood of the Martyrs, the prayers and penances of the Saints, the good deeds of all the faithful, take part in that work which, nevertheless, is perfect without them. He saves us by His blood, but it is through and with ourselves that He saves us. Dear Lord, teach us to suffer with Thee, make it pleasant to us to suffer for Thy sake, and sanctify all our sufferings by the merits of Thy own.

Our Father, Hail Mary, Glory be ...

℣. *Have mercy on us O Lord...*

Can the human heart refrain
From partaking in her pain
In that Mother's pain untold?

THE FACE OF JESUS IS WIPED BY VERONICA

℣. *We adore thee O Christ and we bless thee.*

℟. *Because by thy Holy Cross thou hast redeemed the world.*

JESUS let the pious woman carry off an impression of His Sacred Countenance, which was to last to future ages. He did this to remind us all, that His image must ever be impressed on all our hearts. Whoever we are, in whatever part of the earth, in whatever age of the world, Jesus must live in our hearts. We may differ from each other in many things, but in this we must all agree, if we are His true children. We must bear about with us the napkin of St. Veronica; we must ever meditate upon His death and resurrection, we must ever imitate His divine excellence, according to our measure. Lord, let our countenances be ever pleasing in Thy sight, not defiled with sin, but bathed and washed white in Thy precious blood.

Our Father, Hail Mary, Glory be ...

℣. *Have mercy on us O Lord...*

Bruised, derided, cursed, defiled.
She beheld her tender Child!
All with bloody scourges rent.

JESUS FALLS FOR A SECOND TIME

℣. *We adore thee O Christ and we bless thee.*

℟. *Because by thy Holy Cross thou hast redeemed the world.*

SATAN had a second fall, when our Lord came upon earth. By that time he had usurped the dominion of the whole world – and he called himself its king. And he dared to take up the Holy Saviour in his arms, and show Him all kingdoms, and blasphemously promise to give them to Him, His Maker, if He would adore him. Jesus answered, "Begone, Satan!" – and Satan fell down from the high mountain. And Jesus bare witness to it when He said, "I saw Satan, as lightning, falling from heaven." The Evil One remembered this second defeat, and so now he smote down the Innocent Lord a second time, now that he had Him in his power. O dear Lord, teach us to suffer with Thee, and not be afraid of Satan's buffetings, when they come on us from resisting him.

Our Father, Hail Mary, Glory be ...

℣. *Have mercy on us O Lord...*

For the sins of His own nation
Saw Him hang in desolation
Till His spirit forth He sent.

THE WOMEN OF JERUSALEM MOURN FOR OUR LORD

℣. *We adore thee O Christ and we bless thee.*

℟. *Because by thy Holy Cross thou hast redeemed the world.*

EVER since the prophecy of old time, that the Saviour of man was to be born of a woman of the stock of Abraham, the Jewish women had desired to bear Him. Yet, now that He was really come, how different, as the Gospel tells us, was the event from what they had expected. He said to them "that the days were coming when they should say, Blessed are the barren, and the wombs that have not borne, and the breasts which have not given suck." Ah, Lord, we know not what is good for us, and what is bad. We cannot foretell the future, nor do we know, when Thou comest to visit us, in what form Thou wilt come. And therefore we leave it all to Thee. Do Thou Thy good pleasure to us and in us. Let us ever look at Thee, and do Thou look upon us, and give us the grace of Thy bitter Cross and Passion, and console us in Thy own way and at Thy own time.

Our Father, Hail Mary, Glory be ...

℣. *Have mercy on us O Lord...*

O thou Mother fount of love!
Touch my spirit from above,
Make my heart with thine accord.

JESUS FALLS THE THIRD TIME

―――――――――

℣. *We adore thee O Christ and we bless thee.*

℟. *Because by thy Holy Cross thou hast redeemed the world.*

SATAN will have a third and final fall at the end of the world, when he will be shut up for good in the everlasting fiery prison. He knew this was to be his end – he has no hope, but despair only. He knew that no suffering which he could at that moment inflict upon the Saviour of men would avail to rescue himself from that inevitable doom. But, in horrible rage and hatred, he determined to insult and torture while he could the great King whose throne is everlasting. Therefore a third time he smote Him down fiercely to the earth. O Jesus, Only-begotten Son of God, the Word Incarnate, we adore with fear and trembling and deep thankfulness Thy awful humiliation, that Thou who art the Highest, should have permitted Thyself, even for one hour, to be the sport and prey of the Evil One.

Our Father, Hail Mary, Glory be …

℣. *Have mercy on us O Lord…*

Make me feel as thou hast felt;
Make my soul to glow and melt
With the love of Christ my Lord.

JESUS IS STRIPPED OF HIS GARMENTS

℣. *We adore thee O Christ and we bless thee.*

℟. *Because by thy Holy Cross thou hast redeemed the world.*

JESUS would give up everything of this world, before He left it. He exercised the most perfect poverty. When He left the Holy House of Nazareth, and went out to preach, He had not where to lay His head. He lived on the poorest food, and on what was given to Him by those who loved and served Him. And therefore He chose a death in which not even His clothes were left to Him. He parted with what seemed most necessary, and even a part of Him, by the law of human nature since the fall. Grant us in like manner, O dear Lord, to care nothing for anything on earth, and to bear the loss of all things, and to endure even shame, reproach, contempt, and mockery, rather than that Thou shalt be ashamed of us at the last day.

Our Father, Hail Mary, Glory be ...

℣. *Have mercy on us O Lord...*

Holy Mother! Pierce me through;
In my heart each wound renew
Of my Saviour crucified.

JESUS IS NAILED TO THE CROSS

℣. *We adore thee O Christ and we bless thee.*

℞. *Because by thy Holy Cross thou hast redeemed the world.*

JESUS is pierced through each hand and each foot with a sharp nail. His eyes are dimmed with blood, and are closed by the swollen lids and livid brows which the blows of His executioners have caused. His mouth is filled with vinegar and gall. His head is encircled by the sharp thorns. His heart is pierced with the spear. Thus, all His senses are mortified and crucified, that He may make atonement for every kind of human sin. O Jesus, mortify and crucify us with Thee. Let us never sin by hand or foot, by eyes or mouth, or by head or heart. Let all our senses be a sacrifice to Thee; let every member sing Thy praise. Let the sacred blood which flowed from Thy five wounds anoint us with such sanctifying grace that we may die to the world, and live only to Thee.

Our Father, Hail Mary, Glory be ...

℣. *Have mercy on us O Lord...*

Let me share with thee His pain;
Who for all my sins was slain;
Who for me in torments died.

Jesus dies upon the Cross

℣. We adore thee O Christ and we bless thee.

℟. Because by thy Holy Cross thou hast redeemed the world.

"Consummatum est." It is completed – it has come to a full end. The mystery of God's love towards us is accomplished. The price is paid, and we are redeemed. The Eternal Father determined not to pardon us without a price, in order to show us especial favour. He condescended to make us valuable to Him. What we buy we put a value on. He might have saved us without a price – by the mere fiat of His will. But to show His love for us He took a price, which, if there was to be a price set upon us at all, if there was any ransom at all to be taken for the guilt of our sins, could be nothing short of the death of His Son in our nature. O my God and Father, Thou hast valued us so much as to pay the highest of all possible prices for our sinful souls – and shall we not love and choose Thee above all things as the one necessary and one only good?

Our Father, Hail Mary, Glory be ...

℣. Have mercy on us O Lord...

Let me mingle tears with thee,
Mourning Him who mourn'd for me
All the days that I may live.

Thirteenth station

Jesus is laid in the Arms of His Blessed Mother

℣. *We adore thee O Christ and we bless thee.*

℟. *Because by thy Holy Cross thou hast redeemed the world.*

HE is thy property now, O Virgin Mother, once again, for He and the world have met and parted. He went out from thee to do His Father's work – and He has done and suffered it. Satan and bad men have now no longer any claim upon Him – too long has He been in their arms. Satan took Him up aloft to the high mountain; evil men lifted Him up upon the Cross. He has not been in thy arms, O Mother of God, since He was a child – but now thou hast a claim upon Him, when the world has done its worst. For thou art the all-favoured, all-blessed, all-gracious Mother of the Highest. We rejoice in this great mystery. He has been hidden in thy womb, He has lain in thy bosom, He has been suckled at thy breasts, He has been carried in thy arms – and now that He is dead, He is placed upon thy lap. Virgin Mother of God, pray for us.

Our Father, Hail Mary, Glory be ...

℣. *Have mercy on us O Lord...*

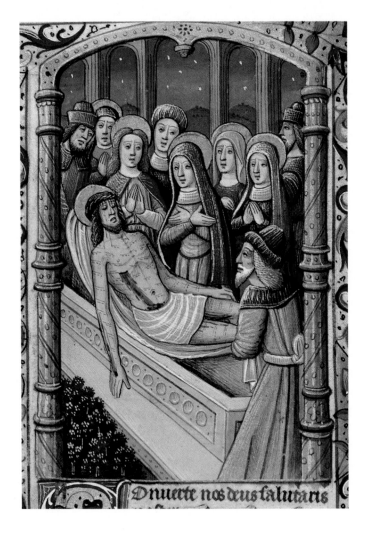

By the Cross with thee to stay;
There with thee to weep and pray,
Is all I ask of thee to give.

Fourteenth station

Jesus is laid in the Sepulchre

℣. *We adore thee O Christ and we bless thee.*

℟. *Because by thy Holy Cross thou hast redeemed the world.*

Jesus, when He was nearest to His everlasting triumph, seemed to be farthest from triumphing. When He was nearest upon entering upon His kingdom, and exercising all power in heaven and earth, He was lying dead in a cave of the rock. He was wrapped round in burying-clothes, and confined within a sepulchre of stone, where He was soon to have a glorified spiritual body, which could penetrate all substances, go to and fro quicker than thought, and was about to ascend on high. Make us to trust in Thee, O Jesus, that Thou wilt display in us a similar providence. Make us sure, O Lord, that the greater is our distress, the nearer we are to Thee. The more men scorn us, the more Thou dost honour us. The more men insult over us, the higher Thou wilt exalt us. The more they forget us, the more Thou dost keep us in mind. The more they abandon us, the closer Thou wilt bring us to Thyself.

Our Father, Hail Mary, Glory be ...

℣. *Have mercy on us O Lord...*

Let us pray:

God, who by the Precious Blood of Thy only-begotten Son didst sanctify the Standard of the Cross, grant, we beseech Thee, that we who rejoice in the glory of the same Holy Cross may at all times and places rejoice in Thy protection, through the same Christ, our Lord.

Our Father, Hail Mary, Glory be ... for the intentions of the Holy Father.